The Wit & Wisdom of

ONLY FOOLS
and
HORSES

D0586867

Splendid
BOOKS

The Wit & Wisdom of

ONLY FOOLS and HORSES

Compiled by Dan Sullivan

Foreword by Sir David Jason OBE

Splendid
BOOKS

Only Fools and Horses was created and written by John Sullivan OBE

Published in 2012 by Splendid Books Limited

Splendid Books Limited
The Old Hambledon Racecourse Centre
Sheardley Lane
Droxford
Hampshire
SO32 3QY
United Kingdom

www.splendidbooks.co.uk

British Library Cataloguing in Publication Data is available from The British Library.

978-1-909109-00-1

Commissioning Editors: Steve Clark and Shoba Vazirani • Coordination: Annabel Silk

Designed by Design Image Ltd.
www.design-image.co.uk

Printed and Bound by CPI Group (UK) Ltd, Croydon, CRO 4YY

CONTENTS

LOVELY
JUBBLY

FOREWORD BY
SIR DAVID JASON

To pay homage to the wit and wisdom of the brilliant dialogue and comic lines in Only Fools and Horses is really a massive tribute to the writer and my dear friend, John Sullivan.

John created the series, wrote the series and nurtured the characters into the ones we all know and continue to love now. With John's untimely death in 2011, I am more than happy to applaud his comic genius and talents through this very funny and insightful book as I consider it a privilege to have been a part of such a wonderful team.

I say team, as it really was an amazing group of people who worked on Only Fools from the cast, to the production team right through the ranks. It really didn't feel right being paid to have so much fun and very often, we were in hysterics for a large part of the day, which didn't always go down too well with the Director and Producer.

One moment in particular was the Batman and Robin sequence. Every time I looked at Rodney (Nick Lyndhurst) dressed as Robin I just fell about laughing and of course every time he looked at me dressed as Batman with my silly little bat ears, he was as equally convulsed.

As I once acknowledged at a BAFTA evening, John gave me the ammunition and I fired the gun and I know the rest of the cast felt that too. John had a great talent in keeping his finger on the nation's pulse and his humour was very much on trend at the time of writing. He took into account the political climate, the social climate and weaved that into the Only Fools' storylines so he really did often speak for a large majority of the nation with respect to the fashion and struggles of its day. His language was street language and he reflected a culture which showed humour and pathos in equal measures. We are all aware of the wit of John Sullivan but his exquisite observations of ordinary life show the wisdom in spadefuls. For that, and the fun we had and the history we made – I just have to say a big and heartfelt Cushty!

Sir David Jason OBE - aka Del Boy

Did you know, 500 years ago this was a green and peaceful area? The old Earl of Peckham had a castle where the Kwik Fit exhaust centre now stands. Flaxen haired maidens used to dance round the village maypole of an evening. And then one fateful medieval day, the Trotter clan arrived in a stolen Zephyr. Before you knew it, the flaxen haired maidens were up the spout, the old Earl had been sold some hooky armour and someone nicked the maypole...

Boycie

ART, MUSIC
AND LITERATURE

As Macbeth said to Hamlet in Midsummer Night's Dream, 'we've been done up like a couple of kippers' - **Del**

I'm a Ming fan myself. He made some wonderful stuff, that Ming. Pity he went and died when he did - **Del**

I saw your face when that Adrian asked me what I thought about Hamlet and I said I preferred Castellas - **Del to Raquel**

Del used to be cultural advisor to the Chelsea shed - **Rodney**

13

Once you've seen one Rubens, you've seen 'em all - **Del**

I'm a great fan of the Byzantine period, myself. I don't think you can whack 'em - **Del**

It's a funny thing, your Lordship, but van Coff happens to be my favourite artist 'un all - **Del**

"Vicky: I was at the Milan School of Art for two years, then I had a spell at the Sorbonne. Where were you?
Rodney: Basingstoke.**"**

15

You could make the Elgin marbles sound like a second hand Datsun - **Rodney to Del**

It's not supposed to get going, it's culture. You don't come to an opera to enjoy it, you come 'cause... it's there - **Del on opera**

"Raquel: I don't know about you but I just love the works of Shaw.
Del: Oh yeah... 'like a puppet on a string...**"**

One day they might make a musical about the history of the Trotter family. Then as a sequel they could do Schindler's List On Ice
- **Rodney**

It's only a bunch of nancy actors doing a play that no one can make head nor tail of –
Albert on Shakespeare

❝Del: What about that poster you showed us, when you was top of the bill with Otis Redding at the Talk of the Town, London?
Raquel: It was Laurie London at the Talk of the Town, Reading.**❞**

He made one great film and then you never saw him again - **Trigger on Ghandi**

You didn't honestly believe all that rubbish, did yer? That you and them wallies were destined for the Albert Hall, the Carnegie Hall? The only 'hall' you lot was destined for was 'sod all' - **Del to Rodney**

Do you mind if I give you a bit of advice, Vicky? See, people round here don't pay £85 for a painting. People round here don't pay £85 for a car - **Rodney**

I'm out there on the yuppy tightrope, me. Nerves on red alert, a beta blocker and a dream, that's me. I eat on the move, a mobile phone in one hand and a pot noodle in the other - **Del**

Mine is not to reason why, mine is but to sell and buy - **Del**

A conscience is nice, but business is business
- **Del**

They're yuppies. They don't speak proper English like what we do - **Del**

My motto is 'West End goods at Southend prices' - **Del**

Del thinks all you need is a Filofax and a pair of red braces and you're chairman of the board - **Rodney**

I'm afraid the company's finished, it's gone. Trotters Independent Traders is no more. It's kaput, it's dead, dead as the emu - **Del**

Asking a Trotter if he knows anything about chandeliers is like asking Mr Kipling if he knows anything about cakes - **Del**

25

We are doing well, relatively speaking. I mean, we are doing well compared to an Iranian gin salesman - **Del**

Oh well, you win some, you lose some. Nothing ventured, nothing gained. It's, well, boeuf a la mode, as the French say - **Del**

26

I don't believe you sometimes, Del. Here I am, trying to clinch a business deal and you've nicked my client's wig - **Boycie**

He wants me to stand in a market, flogging raincoats with 'dry clean only' on the label - **Rodney on Del**

"**Rodney:** They could have you under the Trades Descriptions Act. You call it Peckham Spring but it ain't from a spring.

Del: Yeah, well Sainsbury's, they sell runner beans but they ain't been round the track three times, have they?"

I mean, if some weirdo wants to get it going with half a pound of latex and a lump of oxygen, that's his business. As far as I'm concerned, he could have a meaningful relationship with a barrage balloon - **Del**

Modern business people only speak in initials, don't they? You know, you've got FT - Financial Times, BA - British Airways, GLC - General 'Lectric Company - **Del**

As you're standing on that balcony with your red drink, just above your head in 50 foot high, neon lettering is the word... 'TIT' – **Rodney to Del**

You see, Dave, a losing streak is like joining the Moonies. Easy to get into but a bark to get out of – **Trigger to Rodney**

You need specialised equipment for a job like this. Refined glass brushes, advanced soldering gear. What are we gonna use, eh? Super glue and a bottle of Windolene, knowing you –
Rodney on chandelier cleaning

I've got an early call in the morning. I've gotta get down to Peckham by seven to pick up a consignment of fire damaged woks – **Del**

Well, that is it Miranda. I have discussed the matter with my partner and we both agree that we shall exceed to your delusions – **Del**

When Corrine comes back in here she's gonna find her kettle's been knackered, her kitchen's been turned into a Turkish bath and she's got a Kentucky fried canary at the bottom of a cage... and we're gonna say 'paint fumes did it!' – **Del**

Menage a trois! In the middle of the worst winter for two million years, with the weather man laying odds on a new Ice Age, this dipstick goes and buys out Ambre Solaire – **Del on Rodney**

It's amazing, innit? Everything you buy off him's got something missing – **Boycie on Del**

You see, Abdul's cousin's girlfriend's brother's mate's mate, right, he's a gamekeeper down at one of them private zoos and Monkey Harris' sister's husband's first wife's stepfather, right, works for an animal food company, so put the two together, what you got? A nice little earner – **Del**

There was Mum, bless her. I mean, she tried but her health let her down. Then there was Dad; he would've loved a job except he suffered from this sticky mattress. And there was dear old Grandad, bless him. He was about as useful as a pair of sunglasses on a bloke with one ear - **Del**

Look at the way you dress to begin with. You make a Christmas tree look sombre –
Rodney to Del

Rodney's got some very nice qualities. I mean, she might've been smitten by his rakish charms or his boyish good looks. On the other hand she could be a posh tart fancying a bit of scrag
- **Del**

I wear a trendy trench coat and Gordon Gecko braces. You wear a lumberjack's coat and Gordon Bennett boots - **Del to Rodney**

Your Dad always said that one day, Del would reach the top. There again, he used to say that one day Millwall would win the cup - **Grandad**

I've lived with him for all these years and I thought I really knew him and then something like this happens, some simple gesture and then you suddenly realise what a 100%, 24 carat plonker he really is – **Del on Rodney**

What about the time he was in the navy, eh? Every single ship he ever sailed on either got torpedoed or dive bombed... two of 'em in peace time – **Rodney on Albert**

D'you remember your cousin Audrey? I went to stay with her and her husband, Kevin, for a year. One day, he sent me down to Sainsbury's with a shopping list. When I came back, they'd emigrated - **Albert**

God knows how you've got the courage to walk down dark alleys wearing all that gold. When they see you coming you must look like a mugger's pension scheme - **Rodney to Del**

Freddie the Frog... killed himself by sitting on someone else's detonator... what a plonker - **Rodney**

I've heard rumours Mickey Mouse wears a Rodney Trotter wristwatch - **Boycie**

While all the other Mods were having punch ups down at Southend and going to The Who concerts, I was at home babysitting. I could never get your oyster milk stains out of my Ben Sherman's. I used to find rusks in me Hush Puppies - **Del**

You know what his last job was, don't yer? He was entertainments officer on the Belgrano - **Del on Albert**

Let's face it, Del, most of your French phrases come straight out of a Citroen manual -
Rodney

"**Del:** The French have a word for people like me.
Rodney: Yeah, the English have got a couple of good 'uns, un all."

LOVELY JUBBLY

It was nothing to do with me, Del. I only suggested it - **Grandad**

Of course you wouldn't remember me. Not at my Mum's wedding. I was only a babe in arms - **Del**

Do you remember Rodney? He used to be a little scruff. Look at him now... he's a big scruff - **Del**

It wasn't me Del Boy, it was me brain -
Grandad

I'd have to get done for chicken molesting to bring a slur on this family's name - **Rodney**

He sold his soul for an ounce of Old Holborn years ago - **Del on his Dad**

45

He died a couple of years before I was born
— **Trigger on his Dad**

He was an out of work lamp lighter waiting for
gas to make a comeback — **Del on Grandad**

There's a moral to this story, Del Boy, but for the life of me, I can't find it - **Grandad**

I can almost see my grandad now. Sitting by the fire, one leg on the fender, other one in the corner - **Trigger on his one-legged Grandad**

I used to miss my Dad, until I learnt to punch straight - **Del**

You look like a blood donor who couldn't say no
– **Del to Rodney**

Raquel's got post natal depression, Albert's got post naval depression and Damien keeps chucking toys at my head – **Rodney**

That is England's greatest little sailor since Nelson lost the Armada – **Del on Albert**

D'you realise, by the time I'm 45, son of Del will be 16 and that'll be it, I can hear it now. 'I've got a good idea, Uncle Rodney. I'll go and buy a load of old crap and you can go out and sell it for me' - **Rodney**

49

I'm talking about men and women. You, you're still knocking around with Brownies – **Del to Rodney**

You mean to say that somebody actually trusted you with their property? That's like trusting a Piranha fish with your finger... or worse – **Del to Grandad**

Us being such a law abiding family, we don't really know how to converse with the Old Bill
- **Del**

He tried to join the police force once. It was after he failed the intelligence test to become a Unigate milkman – **Del on Rodney**

He drags me round every pub in the Old Kent Road, holding hands with some old sort with a cough – **Rodney on Del**

51

We were just two lonely people. Arthur was away in the army and your gran had just departed... oh no, she hadn't died, just departed – **Grandad**

You must've spent a third of your life standing in front of mirrors. My earliest childhood recollection is of you standing in front of a mirror. Up until I was four, I thought you was twins – **Rodney to Del**

Rodney, why don't you go in the kitchen and put your head in the food blender? – **Del**

What are you gonna stitch Grandad up with, eh? Found in possession of a forged bus pass? Demanding protection money from the local Darby & Joan club? – **Del to Slater**

"Rodney: Why did you tell me I'd go away for ten years as a special category prisoner, that they'd nicknamed me the Peckham Pouncer, that there was gangs of men roaming the streets, looking to hang me from the nearest lamp post?
Del: For a laugh.**"**

He used to go to work on a horse. And even then he got the sack after two days for wallpapering over a serving hatch – **Rodney on Grandad**

Grandad! It's Christmas night and I am stuck in here with y... I'm stuck in here, watching a film the Germans tried to bomb – **Rodney**

Don't be fooled by him, Rodney. He's had everything from Galloping Lurgy to Saturday Night Fever – **Del on his Father**

> **"Rodney:** Are you trying to tell me that my Dad was a band?
> **Del:** No Rodney, no. Just the brass section.**"**

Well, I can't wait to fill in my next passport application form... Mother's name: Joan Mavis Trotter, Father's name: Herb Alpert and the Tijuana Brass - **Rodney**

They found out they didn't have a patient called Trotter, but they did have a porter called Trotter... but he left two weeks ago with 57 blankets, 133 pairs of rubber gloves and the chief gynaecologist's Lambretta - **Del on his Father**

He was a trainee chef at the Ear, Nose and Throat Hospital – **Del on Grandad**

Take no notice of him. He's an old sailor. He's still got a bit of depth charge lodged in his brain – **Del on Albert**

The last time he had his leg over, Nelson Mandela was in borstal - **Del on Albert**

You dozy little twonk, Rodney. You bang on the roof of my van again like that, it won't be 'Frankie goes to Hollywood', it'll be 'Rodney goes to Hospital' - **Del**

Whatever the subject is, Mum had something to say about it on her deathbed. She must've spent her final few hours in this mortal realm doing nothing but rabbiting – **Rodney**

You take that time you was done for the possession of cannabis. I came here and I told Mum that her little baby was in trouble with the law and it was almost as if I could hear her voice saying to me 'bribe the Old Bill, Del' – **Del to Rodney**

Mum will be there 'cause she'll be wanting to see Rodney, her little wonder baby. She always used to call him that you know, 'cause she wondered how the hell he happened – **Del on heaven**

'Ere, 'ere. I don't wanna worry you two boys, but unless I'm very much mistaken, that young girl out there's up the duff – **Albert**

I've already been through the Adriatic with him once this afternoon. It's like the adventures of a Dover sole – **Rodney on Albert**

★ ★ ★

FOOD
AND DRINK

Pork scratchings? Sounds like a pig with fleas
- **Del**

I've had a lot of sobering thoughts in my time,
Del Boy. It were them that started me drinking
- **Grandad**

What kind of financial advisor goes out to buy an emperor burger and comes back with a cheese burger? - **Grandad**

Pint of lager, Rodney. They'd sold right out of Pina Coladas, Del, so I got you a Mackeson instead. - **Grandad**

I don't know what you're worried about. I've been eating British beef all my life - **Trigger**

I've told you before Unc, elevenses is for wimps - **Del**

"Trigger: I've got a date.
Rodney: Oh, you wanna watch them stones 'cause Del got one caught in his throat...**"**

66

There's everything in here, Rodney. There's sage and onion and molten plastic and... things. It's like Irish night in a delicatessen – **Del on Grandad's Christmas turkey**

You'd nick the hole out of my last Polo if I didn't keep my mouth shut – **Rodney to Del**

If you had been in charge of the Last Supper it would've been a take away – **Rodney to Del**

She had a bit of aggro with the chicken tikka. Mind you, it was a bit rubbery. She was chewing on one bit for about half an hour. I thought she'd end up blowing bubbles with it – **Del**

FRIENDSHIP

When Boycie was born, the midwife held him up and slapped his mother - **Del**

'Ere Boyce. You know this car's a GTI. If you rearrange the letters, you've got yourself a personalised number plate - **Del**

"Rodney: Del, why do they call him Trigger? Does he carry a gun?
Del: No, it's 'cause he looks like a horse.**"**

Have you ever spent an evening in Trigger's flat? It's like having a séance with Mr Bean
- **Boycie**

"Albert: How d'you walk into a 'Mind Your Head' sign? Didn't you see it?
Trigger Of course I saw it, but in those days I couldn't read.**"**

Trig, why d'you call me Dave? My name's not Dave, it's Rodney - **Rodney**

And who are your mates, Del? Boycie, the freemason, a total snob who thinks anyone who's got a pound less than him is a peasant, Denzil is a man who eats porridge with a wig in it, and then there's Trigger, a road sweeper who gives pet names to his teeth - **Rodney**

Trigger? With a computer? Do me a favour, he's still struggling with light switches - **Rodney**

Come on Del, there's gotta be something behind this 'cause Boycie would scalp you if dandruff had a going rate - **Rodney**

You've got to be very careful. I mean, Trig gets very emotional. He's Italian on his Dad's friend's side - **Del**

He's the sort of bloke what buys a tin of baked beans on Tuesday so he can have a bubble bath on Wednesday – **Del on Boycie**

Trigger, you haven't got a family history. You were created by a chemical spillage at a germ warfare factory somewhere off the Deptford High Street - **Boycie**

I can't understand it, Del. I mean, all you've ever done is ruin his wedding reception, almost break up his marriage, flood his kitchen and steal his two thousand pound redundancy money and he goes and gets all silly about it - **Rodney on Denzil**

Mickey Pearce? He couldn't keep a rabbit going with lettuce - **Del**

Parcels attract attention these days. Best to carry it openly, then it don't look conspicious - **Trigger**

You know what happened to the real Trigger, don't yer? Roy Rogers had him stuffed – **Del**

What's the name of that bloke who invented the Dyson vacuum cleaner? – **Trigger**

Give my love to Marlene... everyone else used to – **Slater to Boycie**

He ain't got a few grasses, he's got an entire lawn – **Del on Slater**

According to you and your family, we are looking for a six foot seven inch dwarf, aged between 15 and 50. A white male with Oriental features who's as black as Newgate's knocker... oh yeah, he wears a deaf aid – **Slater**

Oh by the way, if you come across Denzil, tell him I tried to phone him twice last night but I haven't got his number – **Brendan to Del**

I tell yer, if he wasn't so white, I'd swear he was black – **Denzil on Rodney**

Albie Littlewood, my bestest friend in all the world. The greatest pal a bloke could have... and all the time he was doinking my bird – **Del**

For God's sake, Marlene. I might be able to con people into buying my cars, I might be able to convince 'em that you conceived and gave birth in seven days flat, but how the hell am I gonna persuade 'em my Grandad was Louis Armstrong?!!! – **Boycie**

An hour ago, you was 'The Shadow', right, a man of mystery. Now we know your name, your address and your mum's shoe size – **Del to Lennox Gilbey**

I am gonna see if I can buy myself a little doll that looks something like you and then I'm going to burn it – **Boycie to Del**

What? Tell Boycie a sob story? You've gotta be joking. He's the one that cheered when Bambi's mum died – **Del**

"Rodney: Bloody hell, I'm going bald!
Albert: It might not be that, Rodney. You might have a touch of Alopecia.**"**

Once when I was a kid, I was doing my homework and I asked him what a cubic foot was. He said he didn't know but he'd tried to have a week off work with it – **Del on his Dad**

It's a right blinding Christmas this has turned out to be, innit? I mean, some people get wise men, bearing gifts. We get a wally with a disease - **Del**

Haemorrhoids? They were more like asteroids. The surgeon said it was keyhole surgery... he forgot to say it was the keyhole to the Tower of soddin' London – **Denzil**

I'm only concerned with Grandad. Look at him, his brain went years ago, now his legs have gone. It's only the middle bit of him left - **Del**

The doctor reckons that I've got more tadpoles than they've got in the Serpentine - **Del**

I don't know why they want these drug addiction centres, anyhow. I mean, ain't we got enough drug addicts without them recruiting them? – **Grandad**

Look, Rodney's brought you some oranges. I'll put 'em over there, shall I, with the other three thousand – **Del to Grandad**

87

You wanna be a bit more careful about your health, son. In the last half hour you've done so much boot licking, you could be coming down with cherry blossom poisoning – **Grandad to Slater**

There was this woman. She weren't feeling very well. I don't know what was wrong with her but she stunk of booze – **Rodney**

You'd make an Albino look bronzed – **Del to Rodney**

89

Oh listen to me, hospitals do not send home paralysed people by bus... What was it you were after, Del, eh? Sympathy from Lisa or a disabled sticker for the van? - **Rodney**

He's been firing more blanks than the territorials - **Marlene on Boycie**

HISTORY

The way those Germans were carrying on, someone was gonna get hurt – **Grandad on WWII**

Everyone's entitled to a cup of tea, Rodney. I mean, it's in the Magna Carta or something - **Grandad**

Cold? You bits of kids don't know the meaning of the word. You should've been with me on the Russian convoys. One night it was so cold, the flame on my lighter froze - **Albert**

While the nation celebrated, they were hidden away in big grey buildings far from the public gaze. I mean, courage like that could put you right off your victory dinner, couldn't it? They promised us homes fit for heroes. They give us heroes fit for homes - **Grandad on the soldiers returning from WWI**

All the dreaming and the scheming and the chasing and the trying, that was the fun part, y'know. It was like... it was dangerous, it was impossible. It was like Columbo sailing away to find America - **Del**

... one day we were attacked by a kamikaze pilot. He came zooming in towards us - I remember saying to the skipper, 'the way he's carrying on he'll kill himself' - **Albert**

95

That's a bit of history you're holding there, and I mean real history. Not like them Nelson's eye patches Del Boy used to flog to the tourists – **Grandad**

He who sticks his nose into a beehive will get more than a nostrilful of honey! - **Del**

There's nothing worse than Weetabix in a beard, is there? - **Rodney**

We have an old saying that's been handed down by generations of road sweepers. 'Look after your broom' - **Trigger**

I've always been an achiever... I never actually achieved nothing, mind you, but I've always been in with a shout - **Del**

He who dares wins, he who hesitates... don't
- **Del**

I've got this horrible feeling that if there is such a thing as reincarnation, knowing my luck, I'll come back as me - **Rodney**

You should never light a candle when you've got a man with a beard in the house - **Albert**

Trigger doesn't have many friends or opportunity for social outlet. Every weekend he goes to the park and throws bread to the ducks. To him it's a dinner party - **Boycie**

Squirrels ain't got computers but they know where their nuts are - **Del**

I feel like a turkey that's just caught Bernard Matthews grinning at him - **Del**

I've survived all my life with a smile and a prayer. I'm Del Boy, 'good old Del Boy. He's got more bounce than Zebedee' - **Del**

Everyone's a winner, petit dejeuner - **Del**

Please don't give up. Remember what Churchill said, he said 'Up the Alamo!' - **Del**

103

The French have a saying, Rodney. 'Bouillabaisse mon ami' - **Del**

"Girl: What do you prefer, Rodney? Astro turf or grass?
Rodney: I don't know, I've never smoked Astro turf.**"**

I dunno what the younger generation's coming to. They can't even swear without effin' and blindin' - **Del**

104

What a life, eh? Me wife don't love me, me Mum's left me and some bastard's nicked me bike - **Rodney**

There are people on Death Row with more motivation than me - **Rodney**

My image says 'I'm going to the top, flat out.'
Your image says 'I'm going back to bed 'cause
I'm shagged out' – **Del to Rodney**

Running away only wears out your shoes –
Del

I'm on top of the world. I feel like a born again
eunuch – **Rodney**

I am 24 years old, I have two GCEs, 13 years of schooling and three terms at an adult education centre behind me and with all that, what have I become?... I'm a lookout - **Rodney**

You can't trust the Old Bill, can yer? Look at that time they planted six gas cookers in my bedroom - **Del**

It's only E-type Jaguars and Sebastian Coe that make me feel proud to be British these days – **Boycie**

That is the mentality of your spoon fed student type. They walk around all day with 'Steve Bilko' written on their t-shirts, spouting about humanity. When it comes to a fight over a torn fiver, they make Genghis Khan look like a pacifist – **Del**

A right blinding night I've had. I've become a member of a gay club, discovered my brother's a pervo and had a close encounter with two dockers in drag – **Del**

I can now leap out of a Vauxhall Velox 'Dukes of Hazard' fashion, make a chapatti and say 'get stuffed' in Urdu – **Rodney**

It's better to know you've lost than not to know you've won – **Joan Trotter**

I'm one of them that's accepted anywhere. Whether it's drinking lager with the market boys down at Nine Elms or sipping Pimms' Fruit Cup at Hendon Regatta – **Del**

It's an apartment in a complex... a tall complex. Very sophisticated actually. It's got... lifts and everything – **Rodney on the flat**

We live half a mile up in the sky in this Lego set, built by the council – **Del on the flat**

We run a three wheel van with a bald tyre. We drink in wine bars where the only thing that's got a vintage is the governor's wife – **Del**

"Rodney: I saw a movement in the trees.
Del: Of course you saw a movement in the trees. There's a ruddy Typhoid blowing out there!**"**

Would any self-respecting axe murderer pop upstairs for 40 winks and leave his chopper in the sideboard? – **Del**

Del, desperate men on the run don't pop home to borrow a tin opener – **Rodney**

I remember me and Albie Littlewood. We let a couple of tyres down once. You should've seen the palaver it caused. Everyone had to get off the bus – **Del**

Get up as high as you can Del, eh? You might get a tan – **Rodney on Del going hang gliding**

It's easily done, constable. You're walking along the street, your mind on other things. You take your handkerchief out your pocket and BANG! your microwave falls on the ground – **Slater**

Not only have you managed to sink every aircraft carrier and battleship that you've ever sailed on, but now you've gone and knackered a gravy boat – **Del to Albert**

LOVE AND
ROMANCE

I remember me and my missus. I had 18 blissfully happy years... and then I met her - **Mike**

She is a jealous woman, Rodney. A woman scorned. Now, jealous women are no problem to me normally, you know, I can handle all that, but this one is a jealous woman who's an olive short of a pizza - **Del**

It's so long since Rodney had a 'bit on the side,' he didn't know they'd moved it - **Del**

I think in her own way, she loved me. She never used to charge me as much as the other lads - **Albert**

119

S'il vous plait, s'il vous plait. What an enigma. I get better looking every day. Can't wait for tomorrow - **Del**

Trying to rekindle the flame in my marriage is like giving a kiss of life to a rasher of bacon - **Rodney**

In them days, teenage marriages broke up because the husband didn't like The Hollies - **Del**

Sometimes I think you learnt the art of seduction by watching Wildlife on One – **Del to Rodney**

We are kindred spirits, Janice. Seekers of beauty in an ugly, broken world... Janice... get your bra off – **Rodney**

I'm 24, Del. By the time you was my age, you'd been engaged to every bird this side of the water - **Rodney**

"Del: Well, I've been thinking about her all last night, Rodney. She's had a tough old life. Her old man was a right rough house, all the other blokes she's known before that were no better. You know, she's had nothing but bad luck, then she met me.

Rodney: Bloody hell, life's a bitch, innit?**"**

It's moments like this that I wish I carried an emergency capsule of Brut around with me - **Del**

I remember her mum, though. She was a fair sort. Pig ugly but a fair sort. I nicknamed her 'Miss 999' you know? 'cause I only phoned her in an emergency - **Del**

When I approach a bird, she doesn't see the real me; the young, good looking man about town, own teeth and all that. She sees in her subconscious, a white yacht floating on the blue waters of a Caribbean bay. With you, they see a winkle barge sinking off the end of Southend pier – **Del to Rodney**

Stone me, Del. You've been engaged more times than a switchboard – **Rodney**

When he was younger, Del's idea of safe sex was not telling the girl where he lived - **Rodney**

I can't do all that luvvy duvvy stuff. I feel things but when I try to say'em, they always come out... wallyish - **Del**

My love life has taken on a distinctly Russian ambience. Freezing bloody cold and the goods rarely turn up - **Rodney**

Grandad, when he said we was going out with a mother and her daughter, I assumed that I'd be with the daughter - **Rodney**

Rodney can't even give it away, let alone flog it – **Del on Rodney's love life**

Some of your dates arrive by skateboard – **Del to Rodney**

You've had more dogs than Crufts. The other week, Grandad took your suit to the cleaners. They found a muzzle in the pocket – **Del to Rodney**

Let 'em stare. That sort of thing don't bother me, Irene. I went out with a Chinese girl once – **Rodney**

There was Monkey Harris draped over a keep left sign, there was Tommy with the handcuffs on, their two wives were fighting like a couple of strays and this plonker was trying to date the arresting officer – **Del on Rodney**

You meet someone you take a fancy to and within a week it's all wine and roses and 'I'm just popping down to Bravingtons, Rodney' – **Rodney to Del**

I have to live with that wedding album for the rest of my life. How many times have you seen a picture of a bride and groom cutting a jam sponge? – **Corrine**

"Rodney: I've just met the first girl in my life that really means something to me and it turns out to be my bloody niece!

Del: That's why I had to tell you, you see? 'Cause this sort of thing, it ain't allowed. It's... well, it's incense.**"**

Say you had got married to her. Can you see what sort of confusion that would've led to? I would've been your father-in-law. Your mother-in-law would've been your aunt, your wife would've been your second cousin. God knows what that would've made Grandad; the fairy Godmother, I suppose – **Del**

I've got it. What about that tubby girl that lives down by the community hall? She'll go out with you, Rodney, 'cause she ain't got a full deck – **Del**

Tonight, in front of half of Peckham, the bird I told everyone was my girlfriend, stood on the counter and took all her clothes off – **Rodney**

I have just found out that my wife has been lying to me. Every morning she says she's gonna leave me and when I come home, she's still there – **Denzil**

What a turn up, eh? He thought he was gonna pull a Swede and she gets lumbered with a cabbage – **Del on Rodney**

★ ★ ★

The Government don't give us nothing, so we don't give the Government nothing - **Del**

Come on Rodney, I've told you before. It's everything between you and I, split straight down the middle. 60-40 - **Del**

We've always had something missing from our lives. First we was motherless, then we was fatherless. Now we're flogging one legged turkeys from a three wheel van - **Rodney**

"Del: Don't worry. This time next year we're gonna be millionaires.
Rodney: This time last week we were millionaires!**"**

I don't care if it's pesetas, potatoes or Hungarian luncheon vouchers. We're rich! - **Del**

I'm gonna have to pawn all the jewellery again. Honestly, these rings know more about hock than a German wine taster - **Del**

Cassandra, we are talking about Derek Trotter. To Del, 'Market Penetration' means sex under a barrow! – **Rodney**

Come on Rodney. This is our big chance. Eh? He who dares wins. This time next year, we could be billionaires – **Del**

Just think what I could do with a thousand pounds. Fly to America on Concorde, I could buy myself one of those flash Rollox watches... - **Del**

I remember when you got nicked for riding your motor scooter without a crash hat. You only got fined five quid and you asked for time to pay – **Del to Rodney**

"Del: But who's to say I won't sell all this tomorrow?

Raquel: What are the chances of you bumping into a bald headed, anti-apartheid, deep-sea diving Bros fan who has a betamax video recorder, likes Romanian Riesling and whose name is Gary?**"**

He's spent three hours in a stately home and he thinks he's the Earl of Sandwich. You can't wait to get a shotgun and a retriever and go marching across the grouse moors, all done up like a ploughman's lunch, can yer? – **Rodney on Del**

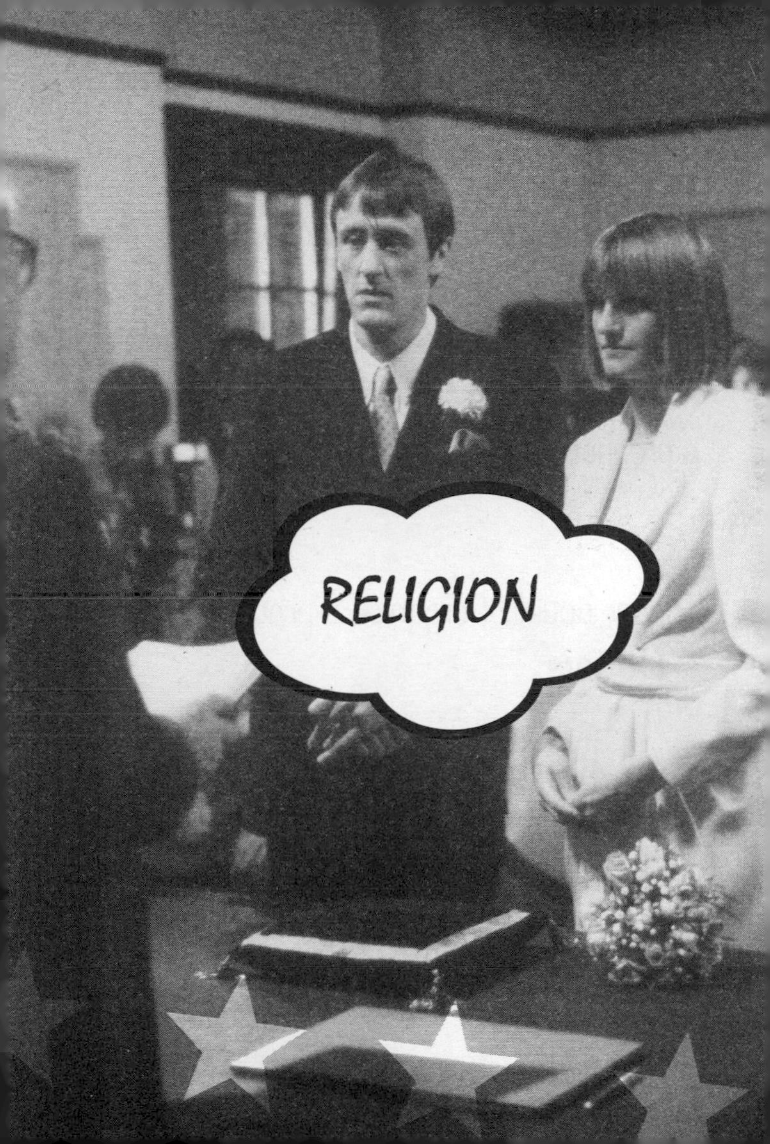
RELIGION

There's cardinals and archbishops, they've been in the business all their lives; they never got a sniff of a miracle. Then along comes Del; he's in the game five minutes and already he's a prophet - **Rodney**

Trigger couldn't organise a prayer in a mosque - **Boycie**

Something happened to me, Rodney. It came like a blinding flash of light. It was like St Paul's journey on the road to... Tobascus - **Del**

I apologise for him, sir. It's his religion. He's an Orthodox tight arse – **Del on Mike**

Christmas is a religious festival. It's meant to be boring – **Del**

"Slater: Whilst in prison, I found Jesus!
Del: What had they fitted him up with?**"**

145

'It looked alright from the outside!' That's what the Christians said about the Coliseum – **Del**

Listen to me. With the money you could earn out of this, you could have that place repaired, redecorated and get Samantha Fox to re-open it for yer – **Del to Priest**

★ ★ ★

"Del : We had Denzil in goal, we had Monkey Harris left-back, we had... we had camaraderie.
Trigger : Was that the Italian boy?**"**

I am a black belt in Origami - **Del**

Kuvera was one of India's premier wicket keepers - **Del**

I was a midfield dynamo, me. I used to play like Paul Gascoigne. The one next to me is Boycie; he used to play like Bamber Gascoigne - **Del**

You can't play draughts on a talking chess game – **Del**

Arthur's ashes? That's the black bloke that won Wimbledon, innit? – **Del**

150

TRAVEL

I've always wanted to go to Benidorm. Where is it? - **Grandad**

Everything was going well, we were having a lovely holiday and then they turn up. Within 15 seconds, some sod's shooting at us - **Boycie in Florida**

Rodney, just get me home will yer. Back to England's green and pleasant land and those dark, volcanic mills - **Del**

It's a well-known fact that 90% of all foreign tourists come from abroad - **Del**

153

"Del: Australia, eh? Where the men are men.
Albert: And so are the women.**"**

The British and the Australians are cousins across the sea. I mean, if your great grandad hadn't been a bloody villain, you could've been one of us – **Del to Australian**

The last holiday we had, the change of climate upset him, didn't it? And we'd only gone to Bognor – **Rodney on Grandad**

I'm going back to the hotel, to have a fiesta – **Grandad**

Only Fools and Horses - The Official Inside Story
By Steve Clark, Foreword by Theo Paphitis

This book takes us behind the scenes to reveal the secrets of the hit show and is fully authorised by the family of its writer John Sullivan.

This engaging tribute contains interviews with the show's stars and members of the production team, together with rarely seen pictures.

Written by bestselling author Steve Clark, the only writer on set for the filming of *Only Fools and Horses*, *The Green Green Grass* and *Rock & Chips*, this book gives a fascinating and unique insight into this legendary series.
£9.99 (paperback)

The Official Only Fools and Horses Quiz Book
Compiled by Dan Sullivan and Jim Sullivan, Foreword by John Sullivan

Now you can test your knowledge of the legendary sitcom in *The Official Only Fools and Horses Quiz Book*, which is packed with more than 1,000 brain-teasers about the show.

Plus there's an episode guide and an exclusive foreword by the show's creator and writer John Sullivan, who reveals some of the mystery behind the much-loved series and just how he came up with some of television's most memorable moments.
£7.99 (paperback)

The British Television Location Guide
By Steve Clark and Shoba Vazirani

This beautifully illustrated book reveals the settings for dozens of top television shows. From *Downton Abbey* to *Doc Martin* and from *Midsomer Murders* to *Doctor Who*, the book gives details of how you can visit the places you have seen so many times on television. It includes details of the locations for more than 100 television series.
Just £9.99 (full colour paperback)

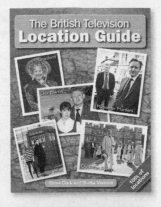

Catching Bullets: Memoirs of a Bond Fan
By Mark O'Connell, Prelude by Barbara Broccoli, Foreword by Mark Gatiss and Afterword by Maud Adams

From the offbeat vantage point of a movie-mad teenager whose grandfather was chauffeur to legendary 007 producer Cubby Broccoli, Catching Bullets: Memoirs of a Bond Fan is a love-letter to James Bond, Duran Duran title songs and bolting down your tea quick enough to watch Roger Moore falling out of a plane without a parachute.

When Jimmy O'Connell took a job as chauffeur for 007 producers Eon Productions, it would not just be Cubby Broccoli, Roger Moore and Sean Connery he would drive to James Bond. His grandson Mark swiftly hitches a metaphorical ride on a humorous journey of filmic discovery where Bond movies fire like bespoke bullets at a Reagan-era Catholic childhood marked with divorce, a closet-gay adolescence sound-tracked by John Barry and an adult life as a comedy writer still inspired by that Broccoli movie magic.
£7.99 (paperback)

A Greater Love
By Olga Watkins with James Gillespie

When the Gestapo seize 20-year-old Olga Czepf's fiancé she is determined to find him and sets off on an extraordinary 2,000-mile search across Nazi-occupied Europe risking betrayal, arrest and death.

As the Second World War heads towards its bloody climax, she refuses to give up – even when her mission leads her to the gates of Dachau and Buchenwald concentration camps...

'A book that deserves to be read' **Daily Mail**

'An incredible story of love against the odds' **Daily Express**
£7.99 (paperback)

Postcards From A Rock & Roll Tour
By Gordy Marshall, Foreword by Graeme Edge

Postcards From a Rock & Roll Tour is drummer Gordy Marshall's witty and wry take on life on the road touring with legendary rock band *The Moody Blues*.

Part memoir, part travelogue, it's a candid, unexpected and often hilarious account of just what it's like to travel around the world playing to sell-out audiences, living out of a suitcase and spending days and days on a tour bus.

If you thought being in a rock band was all sex, drugs and rock and roll, then think again....
£7.99 (paperback)

FREE
DELIVERY
ON **ALL**
ORDERS

To order:
By phone: **0845 625 3045**
or online: **www.splendidbooks.co.uk**

By post: Send a cheque (payable to Splendid Books Limited) to:
**Splendid Books Limited, The Old Hambledon Racecourse Centre,
Sheardley Lane, Droxford, Hampshire SO32 3QY United Kingdom**

Splendid
BOOKS

Splendid
BOOKS

www.splendidbooks.co.uk

Twitter @splendidbooks
www.facebook.com/splendidbooks

www.facebook.com/onlyfoolsbook
Twitter @onlyfoolsbook